D1035024

PANAMA

MAJOR WORLD NATIONS
PANAMA

Tricia Haynes

CHELSEA HOUSE PUBLISHERS
Philadelphia

Chelsea House Publishers

3 5 7 9 8 6 4 2

Library of Congress Cataloging-in-Publication Data

Haynes, Tricia.
Panama / Tricia Haynes
p. cm. — (Major world nations)
Includes index.
Summary: Examines the history, people, geography, economy, climate, and culture of
Panama.
ISBN 0-7910-4977-9 (hc)
1. Panama—Juvenile literature. [1. Panama.] I. Title.
II. Series.
F1563.2.H39 1998
972.87—dc21   98-16070
CIP
AC

ACKNOWLEDGEMENTS

The Author and Publishers are grateful to the following organizations and individuals
for permission to reproduce copyright illustrations in this book:
Art Directors Photo Library; Steve Benson Slide Bureau; Colorific Photo Library;
Michael Holford; The Mansell Collection; Eugenie Peter; Carlos Reyes.

4

CONTENTS

Map		6 and 7
Facts at a Glance		8
History at a Glance		10
Chapter 1	The Isthmus of Panama	14
Chapter 2	Spanish Conquest	24
Chapter 3	The Panama Canal	32
Chapter 4	Political Change	40
Chapter 5	Living in Panama	51
Chapter 6	Panama City	62
Chapter 7	Colon, David and the Islands	73
Chapter 8	Festivals and Folk Traditions	85
Chapter 9	At the Crossroads of the World	93
Glossary		99
Index		101

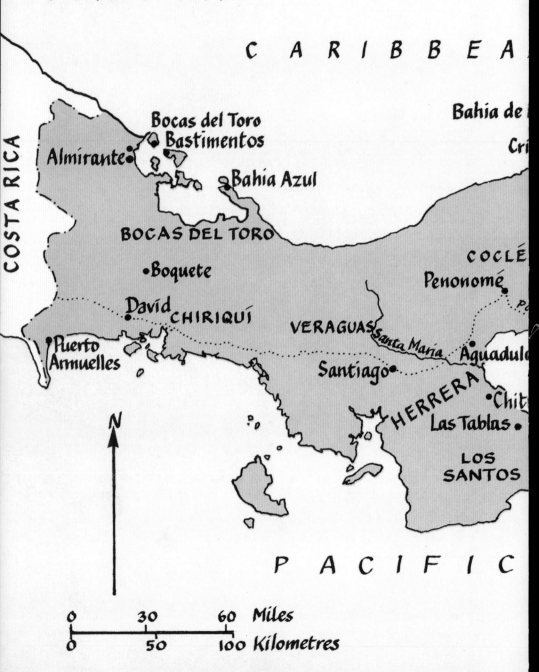

PANAMA

CARIBBEA

COSTA RICA

Bocas del Toro
Bastimentos
Almirante
Bahia Azul

Bahia de
Cri

BOCAS DEL TORO

Boquete

David
CHIRIQUÍ

VERAGUAS Santa Maria

COCLÉ
Penonomé
Po

Puerto
Armuelles

Santiago

Aguadul

N

HERRERA Chit

Las Tablas

LOS
SANTOS

PACIFIC

| 0 | 30 | 60 | Miles |
| 0 | 50 | 100 | Kilometres |

ATLANTIC OCEAN
MEXICO
CARIBBEAN SEA
NICARAGUA
PANAMA
COSTA RICA
VENEZUELA
PACIFIC OCEAN
COLOMBIA
SEA
COLON
Maria Chiquita
CORDILLERA DE SAN BLAS
SAN BLAS ISLANDS
CANAL ZONE
PANAMA
R. Bayano
Panama City
Balboa
Highway
TABOGA
Vacamonte
Contadora
Punta Chamé
PEARL
ISLANDS
Serrania del Darien
La Palma
DARIEN
R. Tuira
GULF OF PANAMA
COLOMBIA
OCEAN

FACTS AT A GLANCE

Land and People

Official Name	Republic of Panama
Location	Narrow land mass between the Atlantic and Pacific Oceans connecting North and South America
Area	29, 157 square miles (75,517 square kilometers)
Climate	Tropical; dry season(summer) lasts from mid-December to mid-April; rainy season(winter) lasts from mid-April to mid-December
Capital	Panama City
Other Cities	Colon, San Miguelito, David, Barú
Population	2,655,000
Population Density	93.3 persons per square mile (36 persons per square kilometers)
Major Rivers	Bayano, Tuira, Santa Maria
Major Lakes	Bayano, Gatun
Mountains	Cordillera Central, Cordillera de San Blas

Official Language	Spanish
Ethnic Groups	Mestizos, Blacks, Caucasians, indigenous peoples
Religions	Roman Catholic, Protestant, Islam, Baha'i
Literacy Rate	89 percent
Average Life Expectancy	71 years for males; 77 years for females

Economy

Natural Resources	Copper ore, gold, manganese, bauxite, coal
Agricultural Products	Bananas, plantains, sugarcane, rice, maize, coffee, beans, tobacco
Industries	Tourism, manufacturing, fishing, offshore banking, merchant shipping
Major Imports	Medicines, chemicals, industrial machinery
Major Exports	Bananas, shrimp, giant prawns, coffee, sugar, clothing, petroleum
Currency	United States dollar

Government

Form of Government	Constitutional democracy
Government Bodies	Executive branch, legislative assembly, judiciary
Formal Head of State	President
Other Chief Officials	Two elected vice-presidents

HISTORY AT A GLANCE

500 B.C. The Volcan Baru culture is established, best known for its life-sized stone statues. The culture is destroyed by a volcanic eruption about 400 A.D.

1501 A.D. Rodrigo de Bastidas becomes the first European to visit the area.

1502 Christopher Columbus sails along Panama's Caribbean coast during his fourth and final voyage.

1510 The first Spanish settlement, Nombre de Dios, is founded at the mouth of the Chagres River.

1513 While on a gold-hunting expediton, Vasco Nunez de Balboa becomes the first European to see the Pacific Ocean (September 26), while on a gold hunting expedition.

1519 The Spanish settlement of Santa Maria is moved to the present site of Panama City and renamed.

1524 Charles V of Spain commissions the first survey for the possible building of a canal across the isthmus.

1574 Francis Drake raids Spanish settlements all along

the Caribbean coast of Central America.

1671 Henry Morgan, a pirate sanctioned by the British government, destroys Panama City. The city is rebuilt but the major buildings of the old city are left as ruins.

1739 Panama becomes part of the Spanish viceroyalty of Nueva Andalucia, later known as New Grenada, which eventually becomes the nation of Colombia.

1746 After years of pirate attacks, Spain abandons the overland route across the isthmus to Portobelo for gold and other shipments from the Americas.

1826 Simón Bolívar convenes a congress in Panama to foster Latin American unity.

1846 The United States secures permission to build a railroad across the isthmus, but the railroad is not actually built for another four years.

1849 The discovery of gold in California brings increased attention to the area, as many people want to cross the isthmus to get to California, rather than sailing around South America.

1850-1855 Building of the first railroad across the isthmus.

1880-1889 A French attempt to build a canal under Ferdinand de Lesseps is a failure.

1903 The Hay-Bunau-Varilla Treaty is signed in Washington D.C. (November 18). The Treaty cedes to the U.S. a canal zone "in perpetuity" and some control over Panamanian affairs.

1904-1914 The Panama Canal is built, one of the great engineering feats of the 20th century. The first ship sails through the canal on August 15, 1914.

1921 Colombia recognizes the independence of Panama after being paid an indemnity by the United States.

1928 American explorer and author Richard Halliburton sets a record by swimming through the canal.

1936 The Hull-Alfaro Treaty limits U.S. interference in Panamanian affairs.

1939 The Panama Conference issues the Panama Declaration, which sets up a maritime security zone extending 300 miles out from the coasts of the Americas.

1941 Panama declares war on the Axis. A large U.S. garrison guards the Canal throughout the war.

1955 A new treaty increases annual payment to Panama by the U.S.

1964 Riots in the Canal Zone lead to a temporary break in relations between the U.S. and Panama.

1968 The National Guard overthrows President Arias. A second coup (1969) installs Omar Torrijos.

1977 A new Canal treaty is signed by Omar Torrijos and U.S. president Jimmy Carter. It provides for the eventual return of the Canal to Panama.

1981 Omar Torrijos dies in a plane crash during an inspection tour.

1983 Manuel Noriega becomes head of the National Guard.

1984 First elections in 16 years put pro-Noriega

candidates in office.

1988 Noriega is indicted in U.S. courts for drug trafficking.

1989 A U.S. invasion force overthrows and captures Noriega (December).

1994 Ernesto Perez Ballardes wins new elections. The situation in Panama remains relatively stable as the December 31, 1999 deadline for the U.S. hand-over of the canal approaches.

1

The Isthmus of Panama

Panama is an isthmus—a narrow neck of land which connects two larger land-masses. It is 400 miles (640 kilometers) long, and only 50 miles (80 kilometers) wide. Panama can also be considered as a kind of crossroads. It links Costa Rica (in Central America) with Colombia (in South America) and lies between the great Atlantic and Pacific oceans. The Panama Canal, almost in the center of the country, enables ships to pass from one side of the world to the other. Before it was built, they had to sail around the tip of South America—a much longer journey.

As it is an isthmus, Panama has two coastlines. On the Atlantic side is the *Mar Caribe*. (In Spanish, the language of Panama, this means the Caribbean Sea.) On the Pacific side is the Gulf of Panama. One aspect of Panama makes it unique: it is the only country in the world where you can watch the sun rising over the Pacific and setting over the Atlantic.

The Atlantic coastline extends for more than 780 miles (1,250 kilometers); the Pacific for 1,019 miles (1,630 kilometers). There are more than 1,600 islands scattered along the coasts, but the best known are the Pearl Islands and the islands of San Blas; the latter are coral archipelagos in the Gulf of Panama, and are composed of thirty-nine islands and 144 islets.

Panama has three main rivers. The largest, the Bayano, flows for 175 miles (280 kilometers). The Tuira flows for 142 miles (230 kilometers); and the smallest of the three, the Santa Maria, for 110 miles (180 kilometers).

Panama covers an area of 29,500 square miles (75,000 square kilometers), which makes it smaller than Portugal. Thanks to the famous Canal, however, it now plays an important role in international and financial affairs.

When Christopher Columbus set foot on the isthmus, in 1502, it was no more than an isolated province of Colombia (then known as New Granada, and ruled by Spain). Three-quarters of the country was covered by dense, impassable jungles and treacherous swamps. Today, the equatorial forest still exists, and is full of exotic plants and animals. It is a dangerous place to venture into without a guide; several aircraft flying over the area have disappeared without trace. Panama is like the banks of the Amazon—beautiful but perilous.

Panama's territory includes two mountain chains: the Cordillera Central, which reaches 10,425 feet (3,475 meters) at its highest point on the extinct volcano of Baru; and the Cordillera de San Blas, which reaches no more than 3,000 feet (900 meters) even at its greatest altitude. This mountain chain extends to the Serrania del Darien (Darien Gap), right on the Colombian border.

The entrance to the Panama Canal from the Pacific Ocean.

Panama's population, like that of many Latin American countries, continues to expand. Over the past seventy years it has increased fivefold. At present it stands at about 2,655,000. Although the figure is small by world standards, it increases at a rate of 3.2 percent annually. Because much of the country is uninhabitable, due to the mountains and jungles, the population is concentrated mainly along the Canal and in the central plateau. This plateau is crossed by the Pan American Highway linking Panama City, the capital, with Costa Rica and the rest of Central America.

The country is divided into nine provinces. There is also an Indian territory on San Blas, called the Comarca. Panama City contains almost one-third of the country's total population. The second largest city is Colón (with 60,000 inhabitants), followed by

David, the nearest town to Costa Rica, with a population of 75,000.

When Vasco Nunez de Balboa arrived in Panama in 1507 with his Spanish conquistadors, there were sixty American Indian tribes inhabiting the land. Today, pure-blooded Indians make up only six percent of the population. They live in the western provinces, the islands off the Atlantic coast assigned to them in 1930, and in the forests of Darien which stretch to the Colombian border. *Mestizos*, people whose origins are part Spanish and part American Indian, form the most numerous group in Panama. The black population comprises fifteen percent of the total and they live mainly in the plantation areas, in the

A view of part of the Cordillera Central, the mountain range in the center of Panama.

towns of Colón and Portobelo, and in the Canal Zone.

Most Panamanians of Spanish and European origin live in the residential areas of Panama City. They form only eighteen percent of the total population. Panama is a mix of people of different origins who have settled on the isthmus and who all live peaceably together. Their religion is Roman Catholic and their language is Spanish, although English is spoken in the larger cities. They are proud of their country, and like nothing better than their folk traditions which date back to colonial times.

Almost everyone in Panama today can read and write. More than ninety percent of Panamanian children receive primary education.

The interior of a Roman Catholic church in Los Santos province. Roman Catholicism is the official religion of Panama.

One-third of the nation's budget is spent on education. Panama is fortunate in having a government which also believes in higher education from which everyone can benefit.

That is not to say that Panamanians are always serious. They know how to enjoy themselves. In their leisure time they take part in a variety of sporting activities ranging from soccer to tennis. Their country provides them with beaches for swimming and water-sports, and mountains for climbing. The mountains provide the country's only cool areas; people who camp there find they need a sleeping bag at night. Many of the mountain villages are reminiscent of Switzerland or Austria, with their alpine scenery.

Panama's climate is tropical—the country is nine degrees north of the Equator. Throughout the year the climate is hot and humid. The temperature averages between 75 degrees to 85 degrees Fahrenheit (26 degrees and 27 degrees Celsius).

Panama has two seasons: one hot and dry, the other wet. Even in the dry period (from December to April) there are occasional showers. This is when visitors like to come to Panama, for it is a time when the weather is more certain. The "wet" season is from April to December. For the greater part of the year, even though the sun shines, skies are often overcast as Panama lies directly in the path of hurricanes which sweep the Caribbean. Storms are frequent in the "wet" season; the rain pours down for an hour or more, and then stops as quickly as it began.

Because it is a tropical country, Panama produces exotic fruits seldom seen in the temperate zones. The banana is one of Panama's main fruit crops. *Platanos* is the Spanish word used in

Panama produces many exotic fruits which could not be grown in the temperate zones. This street stall is selling pineapples and mangoes.

South America for plantains, the giant bananas which are eaten cooked. In the markets of Panama there are also papayas (paw-paw), guavas, custard apples, oranges, lemons and *ciruelas* (plums).

Sugarcane is an important crop for Panama. It provides sugar for export and is also the basis for rum. The country's distilleries produce some of the best rum in the world. In the jungles of Panama there is a wide variety of exotic birds and animals. Some are harmless, like the tree lizards (which camouflage themselves so well that they resemble the tree bark) and the brightly-colored parrots. Others are dangerous, like the poisonous snakes and

20

crocodiles which lurk in the muddy waters waiting for victims. At night, strange sounds echo from the jungle—the croak of bullfrogs, the chatter of monkeys and the squawking of many species of birds.

The intense humidity and high rainfall—about 28 to 57 inches (1140 to 2290 millimeters) a year on the Pacific coast, and 140 inches (3,500 millimeters) on the Atlantic coast—cause plants to grow very big indeed. The colors are bright too. Everything in Panama looks technicolored, from the brilliant red and pink flowers to the beautifully patterned butterflies.

Part of the Panama Canal is bordered by dense tropical jungle, as shown in this picture.

Nowadays, most visitors arrive by air. By land, Panama can be reached by taking the Pan American Highway from Canada, the United States, Mexico or Central America. It takes less than a day to drive from San José (Costa Rica's capital) to David in the west of Panama. Ships arrive via the Panama Canal, calling at Colón and Panama City.

The Panamanian airport, at Tocumen, is 19 miles (30 kilometers) from Panama City. Its flights connect with all the capitals of Europe, with the United States and with Canada. Panama has its own national airline called COPA, and several domestic airlines.

Panama has a wide variety of wildlife and many different species of birds including colorful parrots like this one.

The *balboa*, or Panamanian dollar, is named after the explorer Vasco Nunez de Balboa and bears his portrait.

The Panamanian unit of currency is the balboa, or U.S. dollar, which is divided into 100 centavos. American dollars are used everywhere in Panama. With over one hundred national and international banks, there is free circulation of the American dollar. This makes living and working in Panama much easier today than it was when the explorer Vasco Nunez de Balboa (after whom the currency is named) arrived in the isthmus in 1507.

2

Spanish Conquest

In the early sixteenth century, the country was inhabited by American Indians. They discovered gold in the river-beds and, although they had only primitive tools, they fashioned the gold into the most amazing objects. When Christopher Columbus arrived in 1502, he was so impressed by the gold and silver ornaments which the Indians wore that he said later: "In this land, I saw more gold and silver in the first two days than I saw in Spain in four years."

News of the gold spread, and soon armies of Spaniards arrived on the isthmus, determined to procure the gold trinkets known as *huacas*. This was the beginning of the Spanish conquest. In no time at all, the gold was stolen, and the Indians slaughtered. If Vasco Nunez de Balboa, the young explorer who had made friends with the Indians, had remained in Panama, history might have been different. He might have managed to protect them. But he wanted to discover what lay beyond Panama. With his Spanish *conquistadors* (conquerors) he marched across the country. It was not easy to travel in those days. He and his men had to force their way through

This gold plate depicting the Earth Goddess was found in Peru, but it gives some idea of the fabulous treasures which the Spanish conquistadors took from South and Central America.

impenetrable jungles and swamps infested by mosquitoes. At last, in 1509, he reached Darien. From a mountain peak he saw the great Pacific Ocean and claimed it in the name of the King of Spain.

In 1514 the Spanish Kings appointed a governor for Panama. He was Pedro Arias Davila, known as Pedrarias the Cruel. He quickly ordered Balboa to be arrested and executed on a charge of treason.

Five years later, Pedrarias founded Panama on the Pacific coast. This makes Panama (which, in the Indian language, means "abundance of fish") the oldest country in the Americas. From Panama, armies set out for Costa Rica, Honduras and Nicaragua. The ships of Pizarro and Almagro sailed on to conquer Peru and Ecuador. So the wonderful treasures of the mighty Inca Empire were brought to Panama, having been the cause of much bloodshed. As most of the Indians had been

25

killed, the Spanish *conquistadors* brought in slaves from Africa. The slaves were forced to work in the jungles, transporting gold and silver by mule train to the cities of Portobelo and Nombre de Dios. From there, the fabulous treasures were loaded onto Spanish galleons bound for Spain.

The Spaniards, realizing that others were interested in getting their hands on the gold, built the fortress of San Lorenzo at the mouth of the Chagres River. They believed that this powerful fort would save them from pirate attacks. But the pirates, hearing of the wondrous treasures of Panama, came from England, France and the Netherlands. They sailed their ships into the Spanish Main (the northeast coast of South America, between the Orinoco River and Panama) with their minds firmly fixed on gold.

In 1572, Sir Francis Drake launched his attack on Panama. He set fire to the towns and ambushed the mule trains from which he seized a huge treasure in gold and silver.

In 1671, the most famous pirate of all, Henry Morgan, captured the fort of San Lorenzo and sailed up the Chagres until he reached Panama City. He set fire to the city and left it as a smoking ruin. It was later decided to rebuild Panama City six miles (ten kilometers) away from the original site. This time even stronger ramparts were built to keep out invaders. During the next three centuries no pirate was ever again able to capture it.

After the burning of the city, buccaneers still came to the isthmus in their quest for gold and silver, and Spain was obliged to think of other ways to get the treasures out of Panama. Finally, it was decided to abandon the isthmus route, and to send ships round Cape Horn instead.

Meanwhile, the Panamanians resented being ruled by Spain and fierce rebellions broke out. In 1821, they declared their independence. However, things did not work out as planned and some years later Panama became part of greater Colombia under the protection of Simón Bolívar.

The ruins of the old part of Panama City, destroyed when the pirate Henry Morgan set fire to the city in 1671.

A bust of Simón Bolívar, the Venezuelan general who liberated much of South America from Spanish rule.

But, despite their allegiance to Colombia, the Panamanians still yearned for self-government. Once again there were rebellions. The first took place in 1830; it was followed by uprisings in 1840 and 1861.

While the Panamanians were fighting for self-rule, several speculators were thinking about turning the isthmus to their advantage. In 1698, Scotland had tried to form a colony there, with the idea of establishing a crossing to provide a trade route. But the Spaniards defeated their efforts. It was only during the nineteenth century, after the collapse of the Spanish Empire, that engineers began to think about cutting a canal. Vasco Nuñez de Balboa had dreamed of a passage through the isthmus. Now, at last, it looked as if his dream might come true.

During the years 1820 to 1850, engineers, explorers and businessmen, keen to make their fortunes, claimed they had concessions to build a canal granted by the government of New Granada (Colombia). But none of them gave a thought to the difficulties which had to be faced in the tropical jungles. However, prospectors were not easily put off. They realized that if such a canal could be constructed, Panama would grow into a rich trading area, linking one side of the world to the other.

With the discovery of gold in the western part of America in 1849, many opportunists arrived in Panama on their way to the California goldstrikes. Malaria and yellow fever were two of the diseases they had to face, and many of them died. Still, they flocked to the isthmus. They came in dugout canoes, by mule and on foot. Many never reached their destinations, but died of sickness and disease on the way.

At last the Panama Railroad Company (an American enterprise) began building a railway line from Colón to Panama City, with the permission of the Colombian government. For a while it was profitable. It cost the companies that used the railway the same amount of money as sending their goods by sea, but it was much faster.

Soon, however, people began to lose interest in the railway. Once again, speculators started thinking about building a canal. One of these was the Frenchman, Lucien Napoleon Bonaparte. He

This old photograph shows excavations with a steam shovel during the construction of the Panama Canal.

discovered that no one really owned a concession to build a canal on the old railway route. So he went to Bogota (the capital of Colombia), and obtained permission to build a canal.

He immediately returned to France and sold the concession to Ferdinand de Lesseps. The right to build a canal was now firmly in French hands. Lesseps was the builder of the newly opened Suez Canal (1869). At eighty-seven years of age, when most men have long since retired from work, Lesseps set out to construct a sea-level canal in Panama, as he had done at Suez.

The route followed by the railway had existed since the sixteenth century. Without considering any other route, or a canal with locks which would have been easier and cheaper to build Lesseps began the excavations. After the success of the Suez Canal he could not imagine that the construction of the Panama Canal would cause any difficulties. But it did. By the time Panama became a republic in 1903, much had changed, and the Canal was in the hands of the United States.

Panama today is much more than a canal. It is a busy, modern republic which has earned its nickname of "the bazaar of the west." Communications with the rest of Central America are now easier than ever before, due to the extension of the inter-American highway which carries traffic beyond Panama City.

Although Panama is an independent republic, commerce connects it with the rest of the world. How different modern Panama is from those days in the nineteenth century when Lesseps started building the canal which completely changed the old way of life.

3

The Panama Canal

From the moment, in 1882, when the excavations started for the Panama Canal, the workers (many of whom, including engineers, had come from France) were delayed by dreadful weather. Rain poured down, and the ground was soon so thick with mud that work could not continue. Because of the mosquitoes in the area, there were outbreaks of yellow fever and malaria. Between 16,000 and 20,000 men died.

Money ran out and Lesseps' company went bankrupt. He was sentenced to five years' imprisonment but, because he was an old man, he was pardoned. It seemed as if the canal would never be completed. The French government refused to support the scheme. Quarrels broke out. Debts mounted. Eventually, the construction of the canal was taken over by the United States. The work took ten years–from 1904 to 1914.

In 1902, a year before it was declared a republic, Panama was still ruled by Colombia. This meant that Colombia had to give permission for anything the isthmus people wanted to do. The

Panamanians and the Colombian government quarreled and, in 1903, Panama demanded independence. But the isthmus did not get its way entirely. When a republic was declared, a treaty was signed granting the use, occupation and control of the Canal Zone, including the strip of land on either side of the canal, to the United States.

American money had enabled the canal to be completed, but over the years relations between the United States and Panama were not peaceful. The 1903 treaty which had granted the Americans "sovereign rights in perpetuity" over the Canal Zone was changed many times in favor of Panama, because the Panamanians felt that all their rights had been signed away.

A year later, in 1904, an important health program was organized. This set out to eliminate malarial mosquitoes from the Canal Zone. When that was completed, three major engineering operations went ahead. A dam was built across the Chagres River to form Gatun Lake (one of the three locks on the canal). Then huge, iron locks were constructed. Finally, 8 miles (17 kilometers) of rock which had earlier collapsed in dangerous landslides were hacked out. The difficulties and dangers which had to be faced were enormous. This is why the Panama Canal was recognized as one of the most ambitious engineering feats ever undertaken. And this is why, when visitors arrive in Panama, the first thing they do is drive to the canal.

It cost the United States 380 million dollars to build the canal, which was opened in August 1914. Forty thousand workers, most of them from the West Indies, worked on the construction. Today, the Canal Zone is full of modern houses, swimming pools, and well-maintained roads.

Even long after the canal was finished, there were still problems. The Panamanians wanted total control and, in 1964, riots broke out in protest against America's control of the Canal Zone. It very soon became clear that a new treaty would have to be drawn up.

In 1974, the United States Secretary of State and the Panamanian Foreign Minister outlined a plan to which both parties agreed. The new Panama Canal Treaty became effective on October 1, 1979. It declared that the zone should be transferred to Panamanian sovereignty. This meant that the Panama Canal Commission (a United States government agency, represented by both American and Panamanian officials) would be responsible for the

The construction of Gatun Locks, the largest of the canal structures.

administration of the canal. Panama is set to assume control on December 31, 1999. Until that date, Panama and the United States share the responsibility for the defense of the canal. So, in 1979, the Americans effectively handed control back to the Panamanians who had always considered the canal to be rightfully theirs. There were no more riots and the Panamanians obtained the right to fly their flag alongside the Stars and Stripes of the United States.

The canal is very important to world trade. It links the Atlantic and Pacific Oceans. It is ten miles (sixteen kilometers) wide, and 51 miles (82 kilometers) long and cuts across the isthmus from northwest to southeast.

Over twelve thousand vessels pass through the canal every year. That is over thirty ships each day. Traffic on the canal is between 110 and 120 million tons annually. Three-fifths of it travels in the Atlantic-Pacific direction.

To use the canal, ships must pay a toll. To avoid paying a toll, a ship must sail around Cape Horn, by-passing the canal. Traveling through the canal saves time. If a ship sailed from New York to San Francisco (California) around Cape Horn instead of through the canal, it would have to travel 13,135 miles (22,268 kilometers) further. The journey from Great Britain to Peru via the Panama Canal saves 3,747 miles (9,689 kilometers).

The canal has three different water levels—ships pass through three locks as they cross the isthmus. During the journey, the ships are lifted 85 feet (28 meters). Ships pass through the canal night and day, usually spending between fourteen and sixteen hours in canal waters.

The best places to see the canal in operation are the observatory at Miraflores Lock (ten to fifteen minutes by road from Panama City), and at Gatun Locks. Ships, each flying the flag of one of seventy different nations, constantly pass up and down the wide stretches of the canal.

Ships from the east coast of America and Europe, which enter the canal from the Atlantic, come via Limon Bay, to the west of Colón. As they sail through the canal they pass Mount Hope cemetery, where hundreds of Frenchmen who worked on the canal under Lesseps (and who died of malaria or yellow fever) are buried. Mangrove swamps, once infested by mosquitoes, border the canal. The ships then reach Fort Davis, and arrive at the gigantic Gatun Locks, the largest of the canal structures. There ships are raised or lowered 85 feet (28 meters). Every time a ship passes through one of the locks, the water flows with it, merging

A view of the Panama Canal.

A ship passing through one of the three locks on the Panama Canal.

into the sea. The enormous lock gates have been operating since 1914, and have never needed to be replaced.

All this fresh water comes from Gatun Lake, which is 85 feet (28 meters) above sea level, and so allows the water to run down into the three locks. The lake is one of the largest artificial lakes in the world. Luckily, every year the Caribbean coast gets a tremendous amount of rain, so the lake does not dry up.

Parts of Gatun Lake overflow into the jungle. As ships pass, alligators glide off the banks into the water, and the sounds of the jungle echo over the water. The ships travel on until they enter the Galliard Cut, which at 300 feet (1,000 meters) is the deepest excavation of the canal. It is an 8-mile (13-kilometer) channel cut out of solid rock.

At the southern end of the Galliard Cut ships enter the second of the locks, Pedro Miguel, where they are lowered to Miraflores Lake. They then pass on to the Miraflores Lock, where they are lowered two steps to reach sea level. The Miraflores lock gates are the highest gates on the canal, because tides vary in the Pacific Ocean. Once ships pass under the Bridge of the Americas (built in 1962), they enter the Pacific Ocean.

There are several interesting places to visit in the Canal Zone. One of them is the Summit Botanical Gardens, which contain 15,000 plants from all over the world, including the tropical flowers of Central America. There is also a small zoo in the gardens.

Another place to visit is Madden Forest, which is a well-preserved area of tropical forest and is a good example of how the jungle must have looked to the conquistadors. The Madden Dam is 220 feet (73 meters) high, and controls the Chagres River, keeping water in reserve for the Panama Canal's dry season.

On the island of Barro Colorado in Gatun Lake, there is a nature reserve run by America's Smithsonian Institute. The Institute carries out all kinds of research in Panama, including the observation of sharks and marine life. There is also a Canal Zone museum which displays pre-Colombian art objects, and a detailed model of the Canal. This makes it easy to see the locks and the huge expanse of water in close-up.

When Panama takes full control of the canal in the year 2000, the journey between the two oceans will take even less time, as the canal will have been brought up to date by the most advanced technology. To guard the canal until that time, it is necessary for Panama to maintain a stable government so that it will be ready to take over total responsibility when the time comes. This is the task of the president of the Republic.

Madden Dam, which controls the Chagres River and keeps water in reserve for the Canal Zone's dry season.

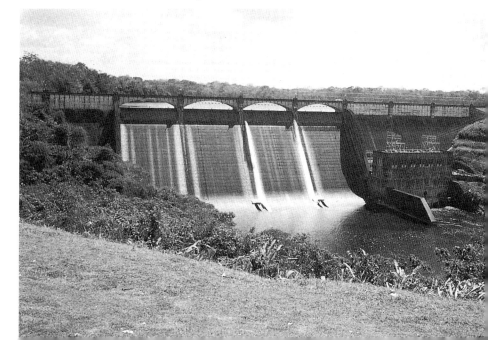

4

Political Change

Ever since the Treaty of Independence, Panama has chosen to remain separate from Central America. The Pan American Highway increased trade with Central America, but Panamanians say they live in an independent republic and are not really part of Central America at all. When the Central American Common Market was formed, Panama did not become a member.

As a republic Panama elects a president to run the country. The president of Panama is elected for a period of six years. At the end of that period presidential elections are held again. Then, he is either re-elected or replaced by a new president.

For the defence of the country Panama has a National Guard. This consists of seven thousand trained men who can be called upon in times of national emergencies. Panama is a democratic republic. Its political constitution is based on the three sectors of government: legislative, executive, and judiciary. The president is head of the executive branch and he is elected by popular vote. If, for any reason, the president is dismissed from office, a provisional

The red, white and blue flag of Panama, with its blue and red stars.

government can be established by a military *junta* (council).

Five hundred representatives are elected in local government areas, and they are responsible for the needs of the people in their region. The National Legislative Council is elected every three years, and the National Assembly of Representatives every six years.

In 1983, Colonel Manuel Antonio Noriega Moreno took control of the National Guard and the country. The first presidential election in sixteen years was held in 1984. In 1987, Noriega was accused of involvement in drug trafficking with Colombian drug cartels. The United States imposed sanctions against Panama and on December 20, 1989, U.S. troops invaded Panama City to restore democracy and to capture Noriega. Noriega was sentenced to forty years in prison in July, 1992. Ernesto Perez

41

Ballardes was elected president in 1994 to serve a five-year term.

As two oceans border the isthmus, it is only natural that Panama should rely a great deal on the sea. Since 1925 all nations have been allowed to register their ships in the Panamanian Republic and to fly the Panamanian flag. Because so many ships register, the red, white and blue flag of Panama, with its blue and red stars, is known as "the flag of convenience."

The Panamanian fleet is now one of the largest in the world, with over six thousand registered ships. Ships registered in the National Merchant Marine provide an important source of income for Panama through taxes, wages and other benefits. They also help international trade.

The Panamanian fleet is controlled by the Ministry of Finance and the Treasury. In charge of this is the Director General of Consular and Maritime Affairs. He is responsible for ship registration and for issuing all ships with the necessary documents.

Panama has seven deep-water ports. On the Atlantic coast are Almirante (close to the Costa Rican border), Bahia de las Minas (which is connected to an oil refinery) and Cristobal (near the city of Colón). The other four ports are all on the Pacific coast. They are Vacamonte, Puerto Armuelles, Bahia Azul and Balboa.

Fishing is one of the country's chief industries, and Vacamonte is the main fishing port. Each port handles a particular product or commodity. Puerto Armuelles is the port for bananas. From there, they are shipped all over the world. Bahia Azul is used for the trans-shipment of oil. Balboa, near Panama City (like the port of

Bananas from Panama are loaded onto ships at Puerto Armuelles and shipped all over the world.

Cristobal on the Atlantic coast) has the latest technical installations and equipment to deal with all kinds of imports and exports.

The ports of Balboa and Cristobal have another great advantage. They are directly connected to the trans-isthmus railway which runs parallel to the Panama Canal, so that goods can be transported quickly and easily across the country.

Since the name Panama means "abundance of fish," it is not surprising that fish should provide one of the country's major industries. These days the Panamanian government is ready to assist any company that sets up a fishing business which creates work for the people. The main catch in Pacific waters is a fish called red porgy. It is medium-sized and weighs between one pound (two

43

kilograms) and five pounds (ten kilograms). It can be seen in all the local markets. Porgy is good for export because it can be frozen and shipped abroad. Striped tuna is another money-maker for Panama.

The country has a fishing fleet of over three hundred ships which are specially equipped for deep-sea fishing. This fleet operates from Vacamonte on the Pacific coast, because the harbor there has facilities for ship maintenance and repair work. The catches which bring in the most money are shrimps and giant prawns. Panama

A typical Panamanian fishing-boat—with visitors on board.

The port of Bahia Azul, which is used for the trans-shipment of oil.

exports large quantities of shrimps and prawns every year. Giant prawns are the country's third largest export, accounting for ten percent of foreign sales. Other fish which make money in the export markets are anchovies, sardines and a local fish called *corvina*, which is eaten throughout Central America. These fish are canned and sent all over the world. Large quantities of fishmeal and fish-oil are also produced annually.

Panama must rely on exports to develop its industries which as recently as 1960 scarcely existed. Today they are beginning to expand. They are supported by two hydroelectric dams, Bayano and La Fortuna, which have been constructed. (The State controls ninety-eight percent of the production of electricity.) Mineral resources are also being looked into, especially copper deposits.

Panama refines oil imported from Venezuela, and re-exports it. The country's other processing industries are based on food products: the canning of fish, fruit and meat. There are also sugar

45

refineries, distilleries, breweries and tobacco factories. The production of cement and building materials has also become important.

Sixty percent of the country is agricultural land. Less than twenty percent is under cultivation; the rest is pasture land. Agricultural methods in Panama are old-fashioned and need to be brought up to date. There is also a shortage of fertilizer, which makes land cultivation difficult.

Panama's main exports are petroleum, bananas (18.5 percent of the country's exports), sugar, maize, prawns, rice, coffee, dried

A banana tree—bananas are one of Panama's main exports.

beans and tobacco. Timber production is also increasing now that seventy percent of the forests which cover the country are being worked. Panamanian mahogany, for example, is plentiful. It is made into furniture or used for construction.

Over the last ten years the raising of livestock has increased. Stock-farming is concentrated in the western province of Chiriqui, and in the Azuero peninsula. Panama's famous racehorse farms, coffee plantations and orange groves are all located in Chiriqui province.

In spite of the fact that Panama's industries have only recently begun to show improvement, Panama has one of the highest national incomes (per capita), in Central America. The Panama Canal Zone, and the Colón Free Zone are largely responsible for this. Panama imports materials such as medicines and chemical products as well as industrial machinery and equipment. Although imports exceed exports, payments for the use of the canal enable the country to enjoy a high standard of living. Panama has low tariffs and taxes.

Colón's Free Zone (*Zona Libre*) is the second busiest Free Zone in the world after Hong Kong. It is administered by the republic, and is extremely useful to Panama. (In a Free Zone, imported goods are not subject to tax.) It occupies 570 acres (254 hectares), and is situated alongside the Panama Canal and the trans-isthmus railway, and highway. There are plans to build an airport, as well as a container port, in the Free Zone. These would help to speed cargo to its destination.

Six hundred industrial and commercial companies do business in

47

The entrance to Colón's Free Zone. The area is separated from the town by high wire fences and patrolled by armed guards.

the Free Zone where no commercial license is necessary. A company simply rents space in warehouses or buildings and can immediately begin activities ranging from sales to American companies, through export of goods, to storage of cargo before it is shipped to other countries. The Colón Free Zone is ideal for trading because it is only 2 miles (5 kilometers) from the port of Cristobal, and 5 miles (8 kilometers) from Balboa and Omar Torrijos airport.

Today, communications in Panama are the most modern in Central America. It is easy to travel from one end of the country to the other by rail or by road; and by sea and air to most parts of the world.

Omar Torrijos airport is one of the most modern airports in Latin America and possesses some of the most advanced technical installations and safety systems. The Free Market, inside the

48

terminal, contains over one hundred shops which sell everything from sports equipment to duty-free bargains.

The airport handles millions of passengers and thousands of tons of cargo each year. It is situated at sea level and is ten miles (sixteen kilometers) from Panama City, and six miles (ten kilometers) from the port of Balboa. Due to climatic conditions, the airport can operate at all times. Pilots do not have to worry about fog, storms or earthquakes; they can fly in and out with complete safety.

A railway journey from Balboa (on the Pacific) to Cristobal (on the Atlantic) takes just over one hour. Today the railway is used chiefly as a cargo route, transporting cargo from one port to another. The train along the scenic route between Panama City and Colón was damaged during the 1989 invasion by the United States and has not yet been repaired.

The total length of the railway system in Panama is 423 miles (677 kilometers). There are also some private rail lines owned by banana companies. The extension of the Pan American Highway, the inter-American route, has greatly improved communications and transportation by road. The highway has been widened and modernized. The final section, completed in 1982, links Panama to Colombia.

Although this route carries a high volume of traffic, it is the best and quickest way of getting across country and into the other countries of Central America. The highway carries cargo to the Colón Free Port, the port of Balboa and to Omar Torrijos airport. Like the railway, the highway runs parallel to the canal banks and, in one hour, the journey between the world's two mightiest oceans—

the Atlantic and the Pacific—is completed.

As well as railways and roads, Panama has a network of bus routes which go to Costa Rica and to towns within the republic. Buses vary in size and shape. Long-distance ones resemble the Greyhound buses of the United States, while others look like large trucks. These are much slower than the stream-lined buses, and make a lot of stops. Travelers may find that they are sharing a bus with farm animals on their way to market!

Panamanians say they have more taxis than mangoes. In Panama City this certainly seems to be the case. There are also "micro" taxis, with cheaper fares than the larger ones.

Travel in Panama, whether by express bus, taxi, train or motorcar, is no problem, even though public transport is likely to be overcrowded.

Living in a tropical democratic republic, where even the smell of the air reminds you that you are close to the hot and steamy equatorial jungle, is very different from living in the world's temperate zones.

5

Living in Panama

Panama has been called a melting-pot, because people of many different origins live there. More than two-thirds of the population are of mixed blood. There are the *criollos,* Panamanians whose ancestors came from Spain and who are the direct descendants of the conquistadors; the *mestizos,* who are part Spanish, part American Indian; the Black people (some of whom are descended from the West Indians who came to dig the Panama Canal); the American Indians who settled in Darien and the islands of San Blas; and various nationalities who came to Panama from other parts of the world.

Most of Panama's 180,000 inhabitants live in two main regions: the Canal Zone, and the two chief cities, Panama City and Colón. Almost one-third of the population lives in Panama City. Few people settled in the eastern part of the Canal Zone, but more than fifty percent of the total population live in the Pacific lowlands (the mountains of the western provinces).

The *mestizos* live in the interior, and the Pacific lowlands. They are

51

The "melting-pot" of Panama—*criollos, mestizos*, black people, white people and American Indians all live side by side.

quite different from the people who live in the canal area. The Canal Zone is populated mainly by Caucasian (white) stock, although there are also many English-speaking Black people, Chinese and Arabs living there. These are city-dwellers who work in the commercial areas. The country people earn their living from agriculture and stock farming.

American Indians make up only six percent of the population. They cling to their traditional ways, earning their living by selling coconuts and handicrafts. One of the three remaining tribes is the Kuna, the islanders of San Blas. They settled first on the eastern Caribbean coast before moving to the coral islands where they

52

preserve their tribal way of life without interference from the government. Of the other two tribes, the Choco live in the jungles of Darien where they live a secluded and peaceful existence. They make their homes from the raw materials of the forest just as their ancestors did centuries ago. Like some of the remoter tribes of the Amazon, the Choco Indians remain hidden, making little contact with the modern world.

The Guaymi, the largest Indian tribe, live in Chiriqui province on the wooded slopes of the central highlands of west Panama, where they earn a living by cattle raising and trading.

Kuna Indian girls, members of one of the three American Indian tribes remaining in Panama.

As the cost of living rises each year, finding a home in the big cities has become a problem. There are never enough homes for everyone. It is expensive to live in apartments in Panama City, and, because foreigners can pay higher prices many Panamanians find it difficult to pay for a home of their own. Panamanians who do not earn high wages have a hard time. There is a huge gap between rich and poor.

Since 1968 social reforms have been introduced to improve living conditions, but the country's wealth is still not evenly distributed. Thirty percent of the work force are employed in agriculture, fishing, and raising livestock. Local industries such as sugar refining, and canning factories employ about 16 percent of the work force, but the workers' wages are still not high enough to keep up with rising costs. The largest portion of Panama's economy is in the service sectors.

Fortunately, because of its free monetary system, Panama can depend on foreign currency by doing business with other nations. As a result many businesses of foreign origin are able to offer employment to local people.

From Panama, most countries of the world can be reached by satellite, telephone, fax, telegram, email and radio. Panama City and Colón have automatic exchanges, so it is possible to dial directly to most countries. Mail deliveries are reliable in the big cities, but less so in country areas. It can take between two and five days for letters to reach the remoter parts of Panama, yet only five or six days for a letter to reach the United States by airmail.

While many country regions look much as they always did, Panama City's gleaming skyscrapers make it appear, at first sight, like any modern city of the world. Yet Panama has not lost its identity. There is still much evidence of colonial Panama in the old part of Panama City, in Portobelo and in Fort San Lorenzo.

Rich Panamanians continue to live in old colonial houses and spacious, modern villas. Others find it suits them best to live in an apartment, if they can find one where the rent is not too expensive. As new blocks of apartments are built, the shanty towns are gradually beginning to disappear. Money pouring into Panama has caused inflation, yet every year attempts are made to improve the living standards of the people.

In the countryside the pace is slower and less competitive. Land has been farmed by the same families for generations, although nowadays many people are leaving for the towns in search of higher-paid employment. However, there is much cultivation to be done in the countryside, and many country-dwellers would not want to exchange their lives in the orange groves and coffee plantations for the faster lifestyle of the city. They prefer their quiet *casitas* (cottages) to overcrowded apartments.

Often the traffic in Panama City and in Colón (the second largest town) is so congested that everything comes to a complete standstill. Panamanian drivers are impatient, with Latin American temperaments; there is a lot of shouting and horn-blowing. Traffic noise in the streets reaches deafening levels but people seem not to mind, even though more crowds and cars converge on the roads every year.

Fortunately, shanty towns such as this one are now beginning to disappear, but there is nevertheless still a gap between rich and poor.

Most office workers begin their day at eight o'clock. They have a two-hour lunch break and then return to their offices, where they work until six o'clock. Shops stay open all day during weekdays; banks are open from eight o'clock until three o'clock, Mondays to Fridays. Panama's time clock is set on Eastern Time (the same as the United States). There are three television stations in Panama. Two are Spanish-language stations, the other broadcasts in English.

Panamanians have a good educational system—about ninety percent of the population is able to read and write. Children attend school from the age of five years, entering primary schools where they learn arithmetic, reading, writing, geography, history and drawing. From there they go on to high schools and, if their grades

56

are good enough, they can go on to university. The University of Panama, in the center of Panama City, is one of the best in Central America. Most educated Panamanians speak English, especially in the main cities and some prefer to study in the United States or Canada. Panamanian Indians speak their own dialects, and Spanish.

These days, medical care in Panama is quite advanced compared with the nineteenth-century situation when malaria and yellow fever were killer diseases. There are hospitals, clinics and modern medical centers with plenty of trained doctors and nurses. Today,

Children getting off their school bus in Panama City—education is compulsory from the age of five.

the water supply is clean but most Panamanians still buy bottled water at their local stores just to be on the safe side.

Panamanian food is similar to that of the rest of Central America, although fish (prawns, spiny lobsters and other seafood) is more plentiful due to Panama's thriving fishing industry. In the country areas many dishes are based on rice and maize, two of Panama's main crops. There are also plenty of *platanos* (plantains) which are used for cooking. Chicken and pork are the most usual meats. Chicken-farming is an increasingly popular business in Panama and, as a result, poultry has become much cheaper to buy. The national dish is *sancocho*. This consists of a thick stew into which everything goes, including chicken, pork and beans. In some parts of Central America goat-meat is also added! In fact, cooks can put into the cooking-pot any ingredients they have available. Like Mexicans, Panamanians also like tamales (corn pancakes filled with meat and vegetables). Beer and rum are both made in the country, so Panamanians drink both, as well as soft drinks. Also available is *aguardiente*, a fiery liquor made from sugarcane.

Sporting activities play a big part in Panamanian life. The National Lottery, controlled by the government, is also a favorite pastime. Everyone buys a ticket, and the winning numbers are drawn at noon on Sundays and Wednesdays. If ticket-holders cannot attend the public draw at the Lottery Plaza in Panama City, they watch the results on television. Tickets are cheap and the National Lottery is very popular. Hospitals, orphanages and other charities are supported by some of the money from the lottery.

Because the weather is good all year round and the coasts of Panama are perfect for water sports, Panamanians can usually be found at the sandy beaches on both the Atlantic and the Pacific oceans. Once they get onto the Pan American Highway they are within easy reach of some of the finest beaches on the Pacific. Between Punta Chamé and Farrallon there are long stretches ideally suited for snorkeling, surfing, and swimming. Gorgona even has a freshwater swimming pool, right on the ocean.

Close to Panama City are the islands of Taboga and Contadora (a twenty-minute flight from the city's Paitilla airport). Then there is the Azuero peninsula, and the beaches of the Atlantic. Spear fishing along the reefs is very popular, as are scuba-diving and swimming.

Fishing is greatly enjoyed by Panamanians, and many world records have been set in Panama's Pacific waters. In July and August there is an annual international fishing tournament in which many nations compete. Fishermen haul in black marlin, sailfish, seabass, amberjack and sawfish. On the Caribbean coast there are snook, wahoo, giant tarpon and yellow dolphin.

Boxing, basketball, car racing and horse racing attract many spectators. Local boxing matches are held almost every weekend. Basketball championships take place from June to September. Car races, which bring in international drivers, are held in February, March and April.

Weekend crowds pour into El Hipodromo, Panama City's

A rural scene—the mountains, lakes and forests of Panama's countryside contrast with the busy cities.

racetrack. There, they can bet on the course and can also buy tickets for La Polla pool, in which they try to pick ten winners to earn high winnings.

But baseball and soccer draw the biggest crowds. From December to February major and minor teams from the United

States are seen in action on the baseball fields, accompanied by the roars of their fans. Soccer, the number one sport in Latin America, has a massive following with fans supporting their particular teams. From time to time international matches are staged, and these receive extensive newspaper, radio and television coverage.

If the people of Panama seek less strenuous activities, there is always the countryside where they can walk, cycle and climb. The Panamanian countryside is very varied, ranging from mountains to lakes and forests, so there are many opportunities for people to relax and enjoy themselves. Contrasting with those peaceful, rural areas are the busy cities where something new always seems to be happening. This applies particularly to Panama City, the nation's capital, where it is hard to keep abreast of everything that is going on.

6

Panama City

Panama City is really three cities in one: old Panama, colonial Panama, and modern Panama. It is the home of 460,000 people who live in the white buildings around the bay and in the crowded, downtown area. On the busy main streets of the Avenida Central and Avenida Balboa, some of the car number plates carry the slogan "Panama, Bridge of the World." This is exactly what Panama is: a link between the Americas. It is also a bridge between past and present, uniting old Panama with today's modern city.

The old city, founded by Pedrarias the Cruel, was one of the most important cities of Latin America. Most of the gold of Peru passed through it, making it rich. Today oil and oil-dollars boost Panama's economy.

Some of the ruins of Panama Vieja (the old city) can still be seen. They include the Cathedral tower and the magnificent golden altar in the convent of San José. When the city was looted by Henry Morgan, a quick-thinking priest saved the altar by painting it black so that it would escape discovery. It did, and Panama kept one of its most famous treasures.

The ruins of the Cathedral Tower in the old part of Panama City, destroyed in 1671.

The ruins of the royal houses, the hospital of San Juan de Dios, and some of the churches show how the city must have looked during the time of the *conquistadors*.

In the early seventeenth century, over three thousand slaves, brought from Africa by the *conquistadors*, lived in the city; and traces of the slave market can be seen today. So can the King's Bridge, which was built in 1620. Trains carrying the treasures of the New World passed over this bridge as they crossed the isthmus on the *Camino Real* (Royal Road).

The old part of the city is a hodgepodge of narrow streets which

63

once had names like Santa Elena—but few names exist anymore. Most have now been replaced. In the modern part of the city, the streets are known by numbers or initials, such as Avenida 5 (Avenue 5), or Calle 1 (Street 1), and U, V, and Y streets, similar to some of the towns and cities of the United States.

Panamanian houses built in the Spanish colonial style of architecture have typical Spanish iron grilles. Those built in the French style are sometimes made of wood. They have elaborate, lacy balconies, more delicate than those of the houses in Spanish style. Both types of architecture are found in the old quarter of Panama City.

Most residents of Panama City prefer to live in new apartments. They like the noisy, hectic streets of the downtown area, full of skyscraper hotels and new office buildings. There, numbered streets make homes and offices easier to locate, but some do have names

These houses in the old quarter of Panama City were built in 1673 in the Spanish colonial style.

A view of the Cathedral in Panama City with the harbor in the background.

like Avenida Mexico (Mexico Avenue) and Avenida Peru (Peru Avenue).

Living in Panama City today is very much like living in a modern American town. There are skyscrapers and new buildings everywhere. The standard of living in Panama has risen too, and this enables people to live a more healthy and productive life. Several multinational companies have offices in Panama City, and more are moving in.

Hotels, with their swimming pools, tennis courts and restaurants which serve all kinds of food, are just like those found in the United

65

The statue of Balboa, on Balboa Avenue in Panama City. It shows the explorer standing on a marble globe and pointing out to sea with his sword.

States. It is often difficult to realize that this is Panama City and not New York or Chicago. Every year new hotels are built, as well as blocks of apartments. Panama keeps on expanding.

Balboa Avenue which runs along the seafront, is one of the main streets of the city. Balboa, the first European to reach the Pacific, is commemorated by a monument on the avenue. It shows the discoverer standing on a marble globe, and pointing out to sea with his sword. Close by is Santo Tomas Hospital, the Panama Yacht Club and the Presidential Palace which was the residence of the

66

Spanish Governors when they occupied the city.

When the people of Panama could no longer defend the old city, they built a capital six miles (ten kilometers) away and surrounded it with massive fortifications. This area is known as the Plaza de Francia (France Square), and is a corner of France right in the heart of modern day Panama City. In the center of the square stands a tall pillar on which a cock is perched. (The cock is a traditional symbol of France.) The monument was built with public funds, so that Panama would always be reminded of the French engineers and workers who arrived in the nineteenth century and who died building the canal. The story is told in carving on the twelve marble slabs beside the monument.

In the lower parts of the fortifications there are a few small rooms. When someone was found guilty of a crime, he was led off to these cells, and left to drown by the rising tide. This deterred other criminals. But in those days times were dangerous. Earthquakes were another problem. Whenever such terrible disasters occurred, people rushed to the churches to pray. They often went to Panama City's cathedral. The original cathedral was destroyed, and the present-day cathedral was begun in 1690, constructed from the stones of the old one, in the old quarter of the city. It has two towers in the shape of pyramids, inlaid with mother-of-pearl. It was completed in 1762. Panamanians attend masses there every Sunday.

Just like other capital cities, Panama has a National Museum, which stands on Cuba Avenue. Although it has a "gold museum" inside, showing some of the treasures of Panama, the best collections are not there, but in the museum in Bogota, Colombia.

The National Guard headquarters and the Administrative buildings are on Ancon Hill. The Ancon project (*ancon* means "cove" in Spanish) is an interesting one. After the Treaty of Independence was signed in 1903, the Americans developed Ancon Hill to aid the canal's defence, and installed equipment to help ship navigation. Today Ancon forms the country's major communications system.

Panama's University, where students study a range of courses from politics to modern languages, is close to Diagonal 3 and Simon Bolivar Avenue. The broad avenues of this part of the city are worlds apart from the shopping centers where everyone fights for bargains. There are several of these shopping centers all over town; the best known is Central Avenue where a free-for-all atmosphere exists. In the downtown areas are Panama City's movie theaters, which show movies in either Spanish or English. Panama also has a National Theater where dance troupes and theater groups perform.

In January and March folk dancing takes place amid the ruins of the old city. At these events the colorful national costume is worn. The girls dress in wide, swirling skirts called *polleras* (literally, "hen-coops"), and have their hair decorated with colored braids. The boys wear little straw hats called *montunos*, white tunics and black knee breeches. Folk dances are performed every Sunday morning at an open-air theater next door to the cathedral.

On Balboa Avenue, one of the city's main thoroughfares, stand the British and American Embassies. There are also consulates

68

Panamanian dancers, in their colorful national costume.

and embassies of other nations, so that if foreigners have problems they can obtain advice and assistance.

Central Avenue leads from the old city to the newer, residential areas. These are on the bay and are called La Cresta, Bella Vista and Punta Paitilla. Many new condominiums (apartment blocks) have been built there because, like any modern city, Panama has its housing problems with many people searching for accommodation. These are fashionable areas, however, and rents are high. Other localities in the city are named Los Angeles, El Dorado and La Gloria.

In the Canal Zone the houses are modern, with all the latest gadgets in true American style. They have fine gardens with lawns kept green by sprinklers. The Canal Zone has its own lifestyle. From there, everyone can see the famous canal, nicknamed "the big ditch." For those who like sailing, the Balboa Yacht Club has its headquarters in the Canal Zone.

Residents of Panama City are lucky to have a National Park right on their doorsteps. Sovereignty National Park was opened in the summer of 1981. What other capital city can say it has jaguars living in forests only a short drive away? The opening of the park means that a large portion of Panama's jungle can be conserved and protected. This pleases the conservationists who would like to preserve even more of Panama's tropical territory.

For some people, shopping can be just like struggling through a jungle. Central Avenue, one of the noisiest bazaars in the world, is like that. Everything from elephant tusks from India to coral from the world's oceans can be bought there. Most goods are sold at duty-free prices. Among the goods on sale are cameras, computers, calculators, video tapes, televisions, ivory, bronze, crystal, brass, watches and leather goods. Local handicrafts, such as the *chaquiras* (beaded necklaces) made by the Guaymi Indians, can also be purchased, as can the colorful skirts known as *polleras*.

Panama City is full of all kinds of shops which sell locally made articles, such as gold and silver jewelry, as well as foreign goods. As Panama expands, more people arrive in the city. For this reason the Atlapa Convention Center and Exhibition Hall was built in 1981. This giant complex (Latin America's showplace) has the latest facilities. It can accommodate up to three thousand people, and offers simultaneous interpreting facilities in six languages.

In order to attract people to their city and to make them feel at home, Panamanians decided to decorate the city buses with typical scenes of Panama such as forests, plains, lakes and mountains. They think this is a good way of showing off their country, and of making life more colorful.

City bus routes are clearly marked, announcing their destinations: Panama Vieja, Parque Lefevre, Via Espana, and so on. In Panama City, you pay when you *leave* the bus, not when you enter. Panamanians shout "Parada!" (which literally means "Stop") when they want to get off. It is as simple as that!

Capital cities are always busy places because people from country

A modern American-style house in the Canal Zone.

areas, and from other parts of the world, all crowd into the capital to find work. This has made life in Panama City very hectic. Everything is done in a hurry. During the rush hours, traffic clogs the streets; and Panamanian drivers are noted for their hasty tempers. Cars on Central Avenue, the main thoroughfares, and many of the city's side streets come to a standstill during the peak periods when everyone is trying to get home in the shortest possible time. Although there is a permanent blast of hooters and frayed tempers, it takes time for the traffic to unscramble itself, by which time the traffic-lights have probably turned red again.

Panamanians eat lunch and dinner much later than people in the northern parts of the world. Like Mexicans, Panama City residents are accustomed to eating their dinner at ten o'clock in the evening; and sometimes they eat even later.

Afterward they may go to the movies or theater, or to visit friends. Panamanians, like most Latin races, like to keep active. Panama City never sleeps. It is a teeming capital, spreading out tentacles like an octopus. But what is it like to live in cities like Colón and David, or on the islands, where life is completely different?

7

Colón, David and the Islands

Colón stands on the Atlantic shore of the isthmus, directly opposite Panama City. It was founded in 1852 and, with a population of 59,000, it is Panama's second largest city. It is built on a geometric plan—a grid system—with numbered streets and avenues crossing each other. This makes it very easy to find one's way around. On Avenida Central (Central Avenue) stands the statue of Columbus and the bust of Lesseps.

The town has a cathedral, some interesting churches (one of the most outstanding is the Iglesia del Carmen, on Street 14) and a Municipal Palace. A few fine old villas remain in the midst of the jumble of slums which sprawl over the peninsula. While new buildings have been erected in Panama City, by contrast, Colón is full of dilapidated houses, badly in need of repair. Each year they deteriorate further because nothing is done about them. Crime is a serious problem in Colón, where daily life is very dangerous.

Consequently, Colón has a run-down air about it. It was, of

course, quite different in the days when cruise ships sailed into its harbor, and passengers spent their dollars in the town. Now that the liners have stopped coming. Colón's economy is suffering badly. While Panama City grows richer, Colón gets poorer. The Hotel Washington, built in colonial times and located at the end of the peninsula, gives a glimpse of the past when times were better and people came to stay.

Colón's "bargain basement" and busiest street is Avenida del Frente (Front Street), which is full of shops (with names like French Bazaar and Jhangimal) where all kinds of goods can be bought. There is also a public market where tropical fruits and vegetables are sold. And this, too, is always crowded.

Most of Colón's residents are West Indians who survive as best they can. Many are unemployed and have few resources, so they are obliged to go to Panama City to find employment.

Without the Free Zone, Colón would have even bigger problems. This area, separated from the town by high wire fences and patrolled by armed guards, brings in large amounts of money each year on imported duty-free goods, which are re-exported all over the world. Over two million tons of cargo is handled annually at Cristobal port, and much of it makes its way to the Free Zone.

Although life is difficult when there is no work, the people of Colón and Portobelo celebrate the Feast of the Black Christ every October. At this festival a life-sized statue of Christ is carried through the streets in a slow, candle-lit procession, accompanied

A typical village in the Central Highlands of Panama.

by traditional music. People come from all over Panama to take part in the singing and dancing in the streets.

Not far from the Costa Rican border and 283 miles (455 kilometers) from Panama City, is David. This is Panama's third largest city, with a population of 75,000. The town has an interesting archaeological museum in the Felix Olivares College. The church of San José is also interesting: its tower is separate from the main church building, and was built in that way to protect the church from attack by local Indian tribes.

Coffee beans—the best coffee in Panama is grown around the Central highland town of Boquete.

David is the capital of Chiriqui province, one of the loveliest and most fertile areas of Panama. It is one hour from Panama City by plane, and six hours by road. Between the two cities are some of Panama's finest beaches. Chiriqui province has some quaint and interesting towns. One of these is El Valle, a *pueblo* (village) situated right in the middle of an extinct volcanic crater. It holds a market on Sunday mornings and people come from all around to buy pottery, straw hats, soapstone carvings and farm products.

El Valle also attracts people from the steamy cities. They find the cooler mountain air refreshing and healthy. El Valle has something else that everyone likes to see—square trees. No one knows why they grow in that way, not even scientists, so many visitors come to see for themselves. Golden frogs are another surprising sight in El Valle; they are found nowhere else in Central America.

76

The Panama Railway cuts right through Chiriqui province, passing trout streams, mountain farms, cattle ranches, and orange groves. To the north of David is Panama's "garden," the Central Highland town of Boquete. Boquete is 3,500 feet (1,266 meters) up the side of the Baru volcano. At that height it is often misty, yet the fertile soil produces vegetables, exotic fruits (mangoes, paw-paws and strawberries), and brilliantly colored flowers. Coffee plantations are situated high up the

Lilies—all kinds of brilliantly colored flowers grow in the fertile soil of the Central Highlands. Every February, the town of Boquete holds a flower festival.

slopes, and Boquete produces the best coffee in Panama.

All kinds of flowers grow there—carnations, roses, lilies and the exotic agapanthus. Panama grows more than three hundred species of orchid, and many of them can be found in Boquete. Every February the town holds a flower festival.

With the completion, in 1982, of the Pan American Highway extension (the Inter-American route), the eastern provinces can now be reached by road, and not only by air or boat as before. From David the highway runs through the province of Veraguas and its capital city, Santiago. The towns of the neighboring province of Herrera have kept an atmosphere of the past, and today still preserve their cobbled streets, and adobe colonial buildings. The *polleras*, the Panamanian women's national costumes are made in Herrera province. Its capital is Chitré, the major agricultural district of Panama, and the heart of the interior. Chitré is a market center for livestock, and has large grain warehouses as well as rice and corn mills.

The capital of the neighboring province of Coclé is Penonomé, the marketing and commercial center of the region. Penonomé has a fine colonial church; but more impressive is the church of Santiago Apostolo (St. James the Apostle) at Nata, with its wooden figures of saints with Indian faces. Nata is one of the oldest colonial towns of Latin America. Near by is Aguadulce ("sweet water"), surrounded by vast stretches of sugarcane fields. This town has a sugar mill, and salt beds which provide Panama with most of its salt.

The Pan American Highway passes through Panama City and

Sugarcane, one of Panama's most important crops.

goes directly to Darien, in the east. Before the extension of the road, Darien was inaccessible; and today the area remains almost as remote and unexplored as when Balboa first glimpsed the Pacific Ocean from its peaks. Choco Indian villages lie deep in the heart of the jungle. The only way to reach them is by boat.

The nine provinces which comprise Panama are all very different. So too are the islands which lie off Panama, in the two great oceans. Two hundred and seventy islands form the archipelago known as the Islas Perlas (Pearl Islands), of which

Contadora is the fifth largest and the best known. The Pearl Islands (most of which are uninhabited) and the island of Taboga are the closest to Panama City.

Taboga, lying twelve miles (twenty kilometers) off the coast of Panama, is called the Island of Flowers. It was once a meeting-place for pirates. It was settled in 1515, two years after Balboa discovered the Pacific. In 1524, Pizarro sailed from the island with one hundred and eighty men, to conquer Peru. Today, with its tiny church and meandering footpaths, Taboga is a small and peaceful fishing village. It has fine sandy beaches where people spend their holidays snorkeling, fishing and diving for coral. There are no vehicles on Taboga apart from water taxis, so visitors can enjoy a feeling of peace and isolation.

Contadora lies 45 miles (75 kilometers) off the coast in the Gulf

The beautiful island of Contadora, 45 miles (75 kilometers) off the coast in the Gulf of Panama.

of Panama. It is reached by boat or by plane from Panama's Paitilla airport. When Balboa arrived in 1513, he christened the archipelago the Pearl Islands because he noticed that the Indians of Contadora were all wearing enormous pearls. Today, four centuries later, they are still supplying pearls and mother-of-pearl to the world.

Like Taboga, Contadora was once quiet and undisturbed, but today it has an airstrip where commercial and private planes land. It is the most developed of the Pearl Islands, and offers the most modern facilities.

The San Blas Islands are composed of thirty-nine islands and one hundred and forty-four islets, which stretch out along 200 miles (320 kilometers) of Panama's Caribbean coastline. The interesting thing about these islands is that no animals, snakes or insects live there—but no one knows why. Even crocodiles and alligators are found only on the mainland. Hundreds of small islets in the greenish blue sea have never been inhabited, and are just a strip of sand which is only visible at low tide. However, even if they are uninhabited, coconuts—the most vital commodity of the islands—grow there.

The Kuna Indians, who fought fiercely for their independence, live on the San Blas Islands. Although several attempts were made to colonize the islands, none succeeded. The Kuna wanted to live undisturbed, following their traditional patterns, and they have won their right to do so. The land is owned by the people and, like most orderly communities, they try to live together in peace. But if there are disagreements these are settled by the chief of each particular island. Officially, the islands are part of Panama, but local laws are administered by the chiefs. Those who get into serious trouble are handed over to the Panamanian authorities.

The Kuna Indians live simple, well-ordered lives. They refuse to marry outside their tribes because they wish to keep their blood pure. They have their own language and customs, but some of them arc now beginning to learn Spanish, the language of the mainland.

An estimated 25,000 Kuna Indians live on forty of the San Blas Islands. Their homes are made of bamboo and have thatched roofs. The Kuna still use *cayucos* (dugout canoes) and have never adapted to modern conditions. They prefer to wear their traditional and colorful costumes rather than modern fashions.

This picture shows a Kuna Indian house, made of bamboo and with a thatched roof.

Even today the Kuna Indians on the San Blas Islands still use cayucos (dugout canoes) such as this one.

Their *molas* (gaily patterned blouses made of several layers of cloth, all of various colors) are highly individual. Each of them illustrates Kuna motifs such as birds and animals. The women wear their *molas* with wide skirts, and wind brightly colored strings of beads around their arms, wrists and ankles. Often they wear gold nose-rings, or the black stripe from forehead to the tip of the nose which is considered a mark of beauty. Some wear the traditional red and yellow printed head scarves, and necklaces of hammered gold.

Kuna girls wear their shiny black hair long until they reach puberty when it is cut short. They choose their husbands themselves and, if the young man agrees, they marry and go to live on the girl's island. That is the tradition of the Kuna Indians.

Coconuts are the Kuna Indians' main source of income, though the men frequently go to the mainland to earn more money, abandoning fishing and the coconut trade to work as laborers in

This mola illustrates a bird, a traditional Kuna Indian motif.

the agricultural areas of Panama. Some find work in the Canal Zone, while others go to the neighboring islands.

As well as trading in coconuts, *molas* and coral, the Kuna Indians, like the other inhabitants of Panama, have many folklore traditions. These are important to all Panamanians because they preserve the culture of their ancestors by recalling their origins.

8

Festivals and Folk Traditions

Festivals are the occasion when many of the folklore traditions of Panama can be seen. Panamanians like nothing better than an excuse for celebrations, and one of the most important celebrations of the year, enjoyed by everyone, is the four-day carnival held just before Lent in Panama City. There is an odd tradition connected with Lent: when the carnival is over, a sardine is buried in a mock funeral at dawn on Ash Wednesday.

A float decorated with flowers—a common sight in Panamanian carnivals.

Everything stops at carnival time, because dancing in the streets goes on for twenty-four hours each day. Monday is supposed to be for dancing, Tuesday for parades, and so on throughout the four-day event. That is not to say, however, that the rules are strictly observed. Floats decorated with flowers, parades, bands, fireworks and surging crowds all fill the streets.

Provincial cities hold their own smaller *fiestas* too. Las Tablas, a city in the interior, elects not one, but two beauty queens, one queen for the High Street and one for the Lower Street, and each queen and her court parade in colorful costumes. Loud music resounds throughout the neighborhood, and everyone prepares to enjoy themselves. Water throwing is a feature of the event, with everyone splashing about like ducks in a pond, as if they had been caught in a tropical storm.

Taboga island holds its own Saint's Day parade on July 16 each year.

Holy Week is another major event in Panama's calendar. In the towns of the interior, ritual dances are customary, in which the dancers wear traditional costumes. Because it is an important occasion, Independence Day (November 3) is celebrated throughout Panama. Anyone can join in, which makes the festivities even more happy and exciting.

Of all the folk traditions, it is those of the Indian tribes—Kuna, Choco and Guaymi—which have been best preserved. The Kuna hold rigidly to their ancestral beliefs, and consider the Earth Mother as one of their most important figures. Although they are now Christians, they cling to some of the old ways, and still practice traditional medicine. At one of their ceremonies, it is customary to drink a strong, fermented liquor which they believe will unite them, and make their community stronger and more powerful.

The Choco Indians—who retreated into the jungles of the eastern provinces of Darien—live simple lives, making pottery and woodcarvings. Little is known of their origins or traditions, whereas the Guaymi Indians of western Panama have more contact with strangers. The Guaymi too adhere to their traditional skills and beliefs. At times they paint their faces with vegetable dye, and the blue coloring acts like a modern-day insect repellent, protecting them from mosquito bites. Both men and women wear *chaquiras* (bead necklaces); like the Kuna, the Guaymi also wear traditional costumes. But the Indian tribes are not the only ones to wear traditional dress. Most Panamanians welcome the chance to put on their colorful national costumes.

The most popular dances at celebrations are the *cumbio*, and the *tamborito*. The *cumbio* has a rhythm similar to that found in some African dances. It is accompanied by drums, and often by guitars and accordions. The *cumbio* is found throughout Central America, but each country claims it for its own, Panama included.

The *tamborito* originated in Spain, but is now popular in Panama. Both dancers and spectators shout or clap while the music plays, to add excitement to the performance. At festivals on a town's patron saint's day and other public events, these dances executed by dancers in national costume are a familiar sight.

Cultural traditions and folklore are part of Panama's history.

Some of the beautiful head decorations worn by a member of the Panamanian National Dance Troupe.

Very little is known, however, about the pre-Colombian period, as the Indians of those times did not use durable materials. The materials used in home-building were the basic ones of wood, earth and leaves, so nothing was left to enable later generations to guess how they spent their daily lives. However, their artistic skills in pottery and stone-carving did survive; and their decorated jars and figurines can be seen in the museums of Central America. It is clear from the objects they left behind that the tribes living in Coclé province were skilled potters.

Although the people of the isthmus had neither metal nor implements in pre-Colombian times, they discovered methods of working their gold, shaping it into most beautiful objects and decorations. Tombs often contained nose ornaments, earrings and other examples of gold objects, bearing the motifs of eagles, snakes and other creatures.

Christopher Columbus himself was dazzled by the glittering display of gold ornaments worn by the American Indians. These *huacas*, fashioned in the shape of gods, bats and frogs, amazed him with their brilliance. How, he wondered, had the people of the isthmus developed such skills? But, without reasoning why, the *conquistadors* seized the *huacas* and melted them into bullion.

Fortunately they kept detailed records of the treasures they plundered. It is those records which tell the story of the precious

Decorated jars such as this one from the pre-Colombian period can be seen in museums throughout Central America; they show that the Indian tribes of the time were skilled potters.

objects. But because the Indians had no written language, the *conquistadors* were unable to document the way they lived. All that survived were a few examples of the gold which they had first discovered in the rivers of Panama.

That precious gold, which they shaped into such magnificent decorations, destroyed the people of the isthmus and reduced them to poverty. Today the few *huacas* which survived have been discovered as far afield as Mexico and Costa Rica. They can be seen in the museums of Central America, and in the marvelous Gold Museum of Bogota (in Colombia). Jewelers throughout Panama sell faithful gold reproductions of the *huacas*, the living legends of Panama's glorious past, when the isthmus contained so much gold that it was called the *Castillo de Oro* (Castle of Gold).

There is more evidence of colonial times in Panama. There was the architecture–the buildings of the Spanish and French colonial periods, including the cathedral of Panama Vieja (1626), the forts of Portobelo, and San Lorenzo, and the church at Nata in Coclé province.

At the time of the conquistadors, the people of Panama were so occupied with agriculture and with making a living that they had no time to consider anything else. While the people of the Old World–Western Europe–were cultivating music and art, the Panamanians were concerned with everyday living. Until 1838 there was not even a printing press in Panama. However, on achieving independence in 1903, Panama began to take an interest in its own affairs. Suddenly people began to take notice of artists, writers and musicians. Poets like Ricardo Miro became

Making modern jewelry—often in the form of faithful reproductions of the *huacas*, made by the Indian tribes in past centuries.

famous. Writers such as Joaquin Beleno wrote about social and political problems. Musicians began to travel the world to play in the concert halls of the United States and Europe.

A form of art known as the "plastic arts" began to develop. This was a new concept of modern art which Latin Americans invented because they wanted to get rid of old traditions, and to have something which was entirely theirs. In Colón, a few Black painters became known for painting in a simple style which had become famous in faraway Haiti.

91

All the while, new ideas were being tested in art, music and commerce. Panama, with its strong cultural traditions, never considered itself a part of Central or South America. It was an independent republic. The time had come for Panama to compete with other nations on its own terms.

9

At the Crossroads of the World

Soon there will be three million inhabitants of mixed origins living in the isthmus. In terms of geographic size, Panama is a small country; but in terms of opportunities it is growing fast. Since independence, Panama has adapted to many changes. Today it is proving that the isthmus really is a meeting-point for all peoples.

Panama has a stable government, and one of the highest incomes per capita in Latin America. Currency is at par with the United States dollar, and can be freely exchanged. Panama is one of the largest banking centers in the world and is often called the "Hong Kong of the West."

Two Free Zones—the Canal Zone and the Colón Free Zone—boost the economy. Like many other countries, Panama's trade balance is uneven, as imports are greater than exports; but with industries growing stronger, the gap is gradually closing.

Above all, Panama is a democratic republic. Having fought for independence it has no intention of losing it now. Panama maintains friendly relations with its neighbors, Costa Rica in the north (which has always had a stable government) and Colombia in the south. Two oceans, the Atlantic and the Pacific, provide the country with fish for one of its biggest industries. Dollars from oil-rich nations continue to pour in.

Panama is at the center of the world. As long as peace is maintained by the government, and fighting does not break out on its borders—as it has in El Salvador and Nicaragua (two Central American countries which lack stable government), Panama will go on expanding and growing richer.

The National Bank of Panama in Panama City. Panama is one of the world's largest banking centers and is often called the "Hong Kong of the West."

Panamanians are free to practise whichever religion they choose. This picture shows a Bah'ai Temple in Panama City.

Today, Panama is more confident than ever before of its identity and its position in the world. With one-third of the nation's budget spent on education, everyone is encouraged to learn and to achieve. Religious freedom is practiced. There are Roman Catholic, Protestant, Methodist, Baptist and Episcopalian churches throughout the country.

More than ever before there is a feeling of patriotism in Panama. Panamanians observe the national flag-raising ceremony every day at dawn, and the lowering of the flag in the evening.

Medical services continue to improve so that people live longer and few babies die. Doctors and nurses are well-trained and caring, though medical expenses are high as in the United States.

95

Communications improve every year and, with the extension of the Pan American Highway, it is possible to travel much farther in Panama, and on into Costa Rica. The national Panamanian airline, COPA, flies to many parts of the world, so people are constantly in touch with other nations who bring fresh ideas and a new approach. Trade fairs and exhibitions are held throughout the year so that businessmen can meet and exchange products, just as the Indians of the isthmus once did.

The republic has also made strides in improving the standard of living. With free exchange controls, more foreign companies are doing business in Panama, and this contributes to the economy.

It is easy to keep up with news from all over the world. Panama has several newspapers. The best known are *La Prensa* (The Press), *La Estrella de Panama* (Panama Star), and the evening newspaper, *La Republica* (The Republic).

Every year Panama City begins to look a little more like the skyscraper cities of North America. With her tall white buildings strung out along the bay, new hotels and apartment blocks, it is hard to know when it will all stop, or if the capital will simply go on getting bigger and bigger.

But the towns of the interior have changed little. More and more people leave them to go to Panama City in search of a job. The government knows that these new arrivals cause over-crowding and hardship, but there is little it can do. People keep on coming to the city because they believe they will find work if they have none, or a better job if they already have one. Housing is a major problem; with people living longer and apartments becoming more

96

A view of Panama City with tall white buildings strung out along the bay.

expensive each year, Panama (like many countries today) has found itself turning to tourism for an additional source of income.

Meanwhile, Panama is looking towards the year 2000, when the Canal Zone will be completely under its sovereignty, and it can run its own affairs without the assistance of the United States. Panama always hoped that a new treaty would cede the canal entirely to the republic. It always believed that the canal belonged to the Panamanians. In 2000 this hope will become a reality. From that moment, Panama will be able to make any changes it feels necessary.

97

By that time the newest technology will need to be in operation on the canal. Modifications have already been made on several occasions to bring the canal up to date with modern developments, and to allow it to cope with the enormous volume of traffic. By the year 2000 the huge iron lock gates will certainly need to be overhauled or new ones fitted. Panama will be responsible for all those alterations and repairs. The Canal Zone will no longer be subsidized by American money, and some of the United States families now living in Panama may leave the area completely. When the Canal Zone, with its American lifestyle (basketball courts and baseball fields), reverts back to Panamanian control, who knows exactly what will happen in a republic dubbed "the Bazaar of Latin America."

It is not always easy for a nation of people of mixed origins to live in harmony, but Panama has managed to maintain that balance, ever since the 1903 treaty declared its independence. The future has never looked brighter. Panama is at the crossroads of the world and, for a growing nation, that is an ideal place to be.

GLOSSARY

archipelago	An expanse of water with many scattered islands.
balboa	Panamanian currency.
chaquiras	Beaded necklaces made by the Guaymi Indians.
Colón Free Zone	Founded in 1953 to provide warehousing, assembly and shipping services; one of the world's largest trading centers.
conquistador	Spanish conquerors.
criollos	Panamanians who are the direct descendants of the *conquistadors*.
huacas	Gold ornaments carved by the ancient Indians of Panama.
isthmus	A narrow neck of land that connects two larger land masses.
junta	Council.
maize	Indian corn.
mestizos	People of a racial mix of Indian and Spanish.
plantains	Giant bananas eaten cooked *(platanos)*.
plateau	an extensive area of raised land.

pueblo	Village.
sancocho	A thick stew that is the national dish of Panama.
Spanish galleon	A heavy sailing ship of the 15th to 18th centuries used by Spain for war and trade.
Spanish Main	The northeast coast of South America and adjacent waters especially in the time when that region was infested with pirates.

INDEX

A

agriculture, 46, 52, 54, 90
Aguadulce, 78
aguardiente, 58
airports, 22, 47, 48-49, 59, 81, 96
Almirante, 42
Ancon Hill, 68
architecture, 64, 66-67, 73
Arias, President, 12
art, modern, 91
art, pre-Colombian, 38, 89
Atlantic Ocean, 8, 14, 17, 21, 35, 36, 42, 43, 50, 59, 94
Atlapa Convention Center and Exhibition Hall, 70
Azuero peninsula, 47, 59

B

Bahia Azul, 42
Bahia de las Minas, 42
balboa (Panamanian dollar), 23
Balboa (port), 42, 43, 48
Balboa, Vasco Nunes de, 10, 17, 23, 24, 29, 49, 66, 79
Ballardes, Ernesto Perez, 12, 41
bananas, 19-20, 42

banks, banking, 23, 48, 54, 56, 93
Barro Colorado, 38
Baru volcano, 77
Bayano River, 8, 15, 45
beaches, 76
Beleno, Joaquin, 91
Bolívar, Simón, 11, 27
Bonaparte, Lucien Napoleon, 29-30
Boquete, 77

C

Camino Real, 63
Canal Zone, 18, 33, 34, 38, 47, 51, 52, 70, 93, 97
Cape Horn, 27, 35
Caribbean Sea, 10, 14, 37, 52, 59, 81
carnival, 85-92
casita, 55
Castillo de Oro, 90
cayuco, 82
centavos, 23
Central America, 16, 22, 31, 40, 47, 48, 49, 57
Chagres River, 10, 26, 33, 38
chaquiras, 70, 87
Chiriqui, 47, 53, 76, 77

Chitré, 78
Choco Indians, 53, 79, 86, 87
climate, 8, 19
clothes, 68
Coclé, 88
coconuts, 53, 81, 83
coffee, 55, 77
Colombia, 11, 14, 15, 27, 29, 30, 32, 49, 67, 94
Colón, 16, 18, 22, 29, 36, 42, 49, 51, 55, 72, 73-75, 91
Colón Free Zone, 47, 48, 49, 74, 93
Columbus, Christopher, 10, 15, 24, 73, 89
Comarca, 16
Communications, 54, 56, 61, 68
conquistadors, 24, 26, 51, 63, 89-90
Contadora, 80
COPA, 22, 96
Cordillera Central, 8, 15
Cordillera de San Blas, 8, 15
Costa Rica, 14, 16, 17, 22, 25, 42, 50, 75, 90, 94, 96
criollos, 51
Cristobal, 42, 43, 48, 49, 74
cumbio, 87
currency, 9, 23, 93

D
dances, 68, 86, 87
Darien, Darien Gap, 15, 17, 25, 51, 53, 79, 87
David, 17, 22, 72, 75-77
Davila, Pedor Arias, 25, 62
de Bastidas, Rodrigo, 10
Drake, Sir Francis, 26

E
earthquakes, 67
Eastern Time, 56
education, 18-19, 56-57, 68, 95
El Hipodromo, 59
El Salvador, 94
El Valle, 76
Europe, Europeans, 10, 18, 22, 26, 36, 68, 91
exports, 9, 20, 45, 46-47, 48, 74, 93

F
Farrallon, 59
Feast of the Black Christ, 74
Felix Olivares College, 75
fish, fishing, 42, 43-45, 54, 58, 80
flag, 42
flowers, 78, 86
food, 58, 72
France, French, 30, 32, 36
fruit, 19-20, 45, 77

G
Galliard Cut, 37
Gatun Lake, 8, 33, 36, 37, 38
gold, 10, 11, 24, 26, 29, 62, 90
golden altar, 62
Gorgona, 59
government, 9, 28, 40, 53, 93-94
Guaymi Indians, 53, 86, 87
Gulf of Panama, 14, 15, 80-81

H
health, 29, 33, 57-58, 95
Herrera, 78
Holy Week, 86
Honduras, 25

housing 54, 55, 62, 69, 73, 88, 96
huacas, 24, 89
hydroelectric dams, 45

I

imports, 9, 47, 74, 93
Incas, 25
Independence Day, 86, 90
Indians, 9, 16, 17, 24, 25, 51, 52, 57, 75, 89
industry, 45-47, 54
isthmus, 14-23, 24, 26, 28

J

jungle, 15, 20, 25, 26, 29, 38, 50, 70, 87

K

King's Bridge, 63
Kuna Indians, 52, 81-84, 86-87

L

La Fortuna, 45
language, 9, 18, 56, 57, 82
Las Tablas, 86
Lesseps, Ferdinand de, 11, 30-31, 32, 36, 73
Limon Bay, 36
livestock, 47, 53, 54, 78
locks, 30, 33, 35, 36

M

Madden Dam, 38
Madden Forest, 38
malaria, 29, 32, 36, 57
mestizos, 9, 17, 51
Mexico, 22, 90

Miraflores, Lake, Lock, 36, 38
Miro, Ricardo, 90
molas, 83, 84
montunos, 68
Morgan, Henry, 10, 26, 62
Mount Hope cemetery, 36

N

Nata, 78, 90
National Assembly of Representatives, 41
National Guard, 40, 68
National Legislative Council, 41
National Lottery, 58
New Granada (*see* Colombia)
newspapers, 61, 96
Nicaragua, 25, 94
Noriega, Manuel, 12, 41

O

oil, 42, 45, 62
Omar Torrijos airport, 48-49

P

Pacific Ocean, 8, 10, 14, 21, 25, 35, 38, 42, 44, 50, 59, 66, 79, 94
Paitilla airport, 59
Pan American Highway, 16, 22, 31, 40, 49, 59, 78, 96
Panama Canal, 14, 32-39, 43, 47
Panama Canal Commission, 34
Panama Canal, construction of, 11
Panama Canal Treaty, 11, 33, 34
Panama City, 8, 10, 16, 22, 26, 29, 49, 50, 51, 54, 55, 57, 59, 62-72, 74, 76
Panama Railroad Company, 29

Pearl Islands, 15, 79-81
Pedrarias the Cruel, 25, 62
Pedro Miguel Lock, 38
Penonomé, 78
pirates, 26, 80
plantains (*platanos*), 19-20, 58
plants, 15, 20, 21, 38
plateau, 16
polleras, 68, 70, 78
population, 9, 16, 17, 18, 51, 62, 73, 75
Portobelo, 18, 26, 55, 74
Puerto Armuelles, 42
Punta Chamé, 59

R
rainfall, 19, 21, 32
religion, 9, 18, 95
revolt, 27, 28
rum, 20, 58

S
San Blas Islands, 15, 51, 52, 81, 82
sancocho, 58
San José, 22, 62, 75
San Juan de Dios, 63
San Lorenzo, 26, 55
Santa Maria River, 8, 10, 15
Santiago, 78
Serrania del Darien, 15
slaves, 26, 83
Smithsonian Insititute, 38
South America, 8, 14, 20
Spain, Spaniards, 11, 15, 17, 18, 24-31, 51, 56, 64
sports, 19, 58-61

sugar, 20
Summit Botanical Gardens, 38

T
Taboga, 5, 80
tamales, 58
tamborito, 87
telephone, 54
television, 56, 58, 61
Tocumen, 22
Torrijos, Omar, 12
trans-isthmus railway, 11, 43, 47
transport, 22, 29, 48-50, 77, 80
Treaty of Independence, 40, 68
Tuira River, 8, 15

U
United States, 9, 11, 12, 22, 29, 31, 32, 33, 35, 36, 41, 49, 54, 57, 64, 68, 91, 93, 95, 97, 98
University of Panama, 57, 68

V
Vacamonte, 42, 44
Veraguas, 78
Volcan Baru, 10, 15
volcanoes, 10

W
wildlife, 15, 20-21, 38, 81

Y
yellow fever, 29, 32, 36, 57